Drawn to Discipleship

Dr. Amanda Goodson

AMANDA GOODSON

ISBN-13: 978-0997875744

ISBN-10: 0997875747

Printed in the U.S.A.

Second Edition

CONTENTS

ACKNOWLEDGMENTS

Thank You, God, for allowing me to serve You in such a manner as is pleasing to You. I pray that I will find favor in Your sight as I share these stories with others and that they may also be blessed. I am grateful for my family, for their dedication to me, and all that God has allowed me to do.

Bishop Bobby R. Best and Trinity Temple Tucson, thanks for the inspiration.

Thank you to Diane Snell for being a significant contributor to this ministry effort.

Dr. Amanda Goodson

INTRODUCTION

God, as our heavenly Father, wants to teach us about His way, will and desire for our lives. From the moment that God gives us His breath of life, we have the opportunity to experience oneness with Him and we can learn more about Him every day. In the Amplified version of The Bible, in Exodus 33:13 Moses prayed that if he had found favor in God's sight that He may show Moses the way to know God–to progressively become more deeply and intimately acquainted with Him. Moses wanted to know God so well that he would perceive and recognize and understand more strongly and clearly who God is. He further requested that he may be acknowledged to find favor in God's sight...by God's presence going with him and the people of Israel.

For us today, we too may come know God deeply and strongly; acknowledging His presence clearly through Jesus Christ, His Son. As disciples (learners, followers and kingdom sons), we can learn and participate in God's kingdom right now!

This book, *Drawn to Discipleship,* comprises a daily journey of revelation through prayer, in to that place where we can become better disciples of God and reach a place where we find divine learning, impartation and inspiration. Every learner should desire to pray better and become comfortable doing so every day.

This daily walk will gently guide the reader in taking a practical and applicable journey of followership in order to reach Christ's goal for all to know God. The intent of this book, as with my other 21 Days of Prayer books, is that the reader be able to accomplish this by utilizing relevant stories that demonstrate how to live and are made better because of a true relationship with Jesus Christ the Savior.

It isn't always necessary to sound deep and spiritual to learn the how God thinks, and conversely, to be heard. We should come to God as children and learn of Him. Our prayer lives and daily walk should be a reflection of that learning. Simply put, our prayers should be presented with a spirit that is humble and yet straightforward. Reverent, in that we must always come before God in a way that is respectful and with a spirit of worship. Specific, in that we should be clear in stating precisely what the prayer references. Trusting, in that we are to fully believe and know that God is who He says He is, and that He will do precisely what His Word promises He will do. Learned, following His ways and seeing His miracles, signs and wonders.

I invite you to take this daily journey and see how your life can and will be transformed through prayer. It is guaranteed that, through a daily commitment to prayer, your life will be changed, your relationship with God will be enhanced, and you will see the difference this makes in your life.

1 WHAT IS DISCIPLESHIP?

Purpose:
The importance of walking in love as a disciple of Jesus Christ.

Hearing the Word:
Ephesians 5:1-2
"Follow God's example, therefore, as dearly loved children, and walk in the way of love, just as Christ loved us and gave himself up for us as a fragrant offering and sacrifice to God."

Follow God's example and walk in the way of love! What a directive! According to John 15:13, "Greater love has no one than this: to lay down one's life for one's friends. You are my friends if you do what I command. I no longer call you servants, because a servant does not know his master's business. Instead,

1

I have called you friends, for everything that I learned from my Father I have made known to you." We know the truth of discipleship because Jesus has shared everything he learned from God with us! God is love. This is the emphatic statement in 1 John 4:8, "Whoever does not love does not know God, because God is love." God has shown His love for us by giving Christ as the ultimate and final sacrifice.

God has given to all mankind the greatest example of a true disciple, His son Jesus Christ. God so loved us that he gave His son Jesus for our salvation. It is this great love that we return to God by inviting the "lost" into a kingdom relationship with him. We as dearly loved children must walk in the way of love emulating Christ, God's only begotten son. Scripture, in John 3:16 states "For God so loved the world that He gave His one and only Son, that whoever believes in him shall not perish but have eternal life. For God did not send his Son into the world to condemn the world, but to save the world through him."

Jesus taught by example the ways and will of God to all who would listen.

He chose His first disciples with a promise to make them "fishers of men." In Mark 1:16-17 it states, "As Jesus walked beside the Sea of Galilee, He saw Simon and his brother Andrew casting a net into the lake, for they were fishermen. "Come, follow Me," Jesus said, "and I will send you out to fish for people." It was truly an invitation to discipleship. Jesus spoke plainly and clearly to them, using terminology they would understand. He utilized the vernacular of the day for the situation at hand making it clear to them that they would no longer catch fish, but would be elevated to a higher calling–serving and saving the lost among men.

Our first venture into discipleship occurred when we learned to follow the rules and orders our parents gave us. From early childhood we learned to stop running in the house, do our chores, eat our food, share our toys and heed the protective warnings of our elders. We learned respect and adoration for our loved ones. We learned to sympathize and have compassion for all.

Both church and the world teach us what love is and is not. As we grow into adulthood we know that love teaches, corrects, rebukes and trains us in the way we should grow up. Church folk learn to trust God from being surrounded by people who constantly speak positively about doing the same. The family unit is a powerful example of a great environmental setting for teaching disciples. As love directs the growth and maturity of the individual, Scripture (The Word of God) directs the growth and maturity of the disciple.

The Bible says in Proverbs 22:6 "Train up a child in the way he should go; and when he is old, he will not depart from it. Jesus returned to the synagogue in Nazareth, the city where He was a child. He followed the customs of the church to which He had previous learning. It was custom that the scroll was read prior to the preaching on the Sabbath. Jesus reading the Scripture from the Isaiah scroll was not news or new for that service. Theologians believe that on this particular morning Jesus took the scroll and read the following scripture from Isaiah (found in Luke 4:16-21); to the people sitting in the synagogue on that Sunday.

Jesus went to Nazareth, where He had been brought up, and on the Sabbath He went into the synagogue, as was His custom. He stood up to read and the scroll of the prophet Isaiah was handed to him. Unrolling it, He found the place where it is written:

"The Spirit of the Lord is on me; because he has anointed me to proclaim good news to the poor. He has sent me to proclaim freedom for the prisoners, and recovery of sight for the blind. To set the oppressed free, to proclaim the year of the Lord's favor." Then He rolled up the scroll, gave it back to the attendant and sat down.

Jesus then sat down to deliver the message for that service. These were all customary procedures that were taught to every Jewish child of that day. It was customary that the one who read the scroll then delivered the message for the day. Jesus knew and followed the order of service. He would also teach His disciples (then and now) the true meaning of discipleship, love, obedience, submission, order and authority.

Discipleship is a multi-faceted role in the church organizational structure. To gain a better understanding of discipleship we will review our understanding of the term 'disciple.' *The American Heritage College Dictionary* gives the following definition of the word "Disciple:" One who assists in spreading the teachings of another: An active adherent, as of a movement. The synonyms listed for the word Disciple include: apostle, follower. Defines the word disciple as a scholar, sometimes applied to the followers of John the Baptist (Matthew 9:14), and of the Pharisees (22:16), but principally to the following of Christ.

A Disciple of Christ is one who:

1. Believes His doctrine,
2. Rests on His sacrifice,
3. Imbibes His spirit, and
4. Imitates His example (Matthew 10:24, Luke 14:26, 27.33; John 6:69).

The Hebrew meaning of disciple is pupil or student.

The disciples were people who chose to follow Jesus and to listen to His teaching. They called Him *rabbi,* or teacher. The twelve disciples were followers of Jesus.

The chosen were:

- Simon Peter - Fisherman, son of John
- Andrew - Fisherman, son of John and Peter's brother
- James - Fisherman, son of Zebedee, son of Boanerges (thunder)
- John - Fisherman, son of Zebedee, Boanerges (thunder), brother of James
- Philip - From Bethsaida
- Matthew - tax collector, son of Alphaeus
- Nathaniel (Bartholomew) - from Cana, a "true Israelite"
- Thomas
- James, son of Alphaeus
- Simon, the Zealot

Disciple is the physical person whose activities are described by the word "discipleship." Jesus was able to interact with and teach His disciples (and all mankind) how to humble themselves before God. He taught them by example how to interact and respond to the calling and commands of God. Ever so important, Jesus taught all believers how to humble themselves before God and carry out the will and purpose God has for humanity.

The process of becoming a disciple culminates with an active work called discipleship. Disciples must prepare for the mission ahead. Jesus spent three years preparing His disciples for the lifelong task ahead of them. They were sent out to seek out those in need of a greater understanding of God's power, love, and authority over mankind. Jesus knew the purpose of His mission.

He said, "I did not come to do away with the law but to save the lost."

This is the focus and intent of discipleship: to save the lost. A good example of a discipleship system is the education system in the United States. The student receives twelve years of study to learn all of the basic education requirements. Upon graduation they decide to prepare themselves for future endeavors by attending schools to obtain a higher, more specific foundation in their chosen field. Universities provide specific, centered training, which allows the graduating students to pursue careers within their chosen area. Jesus' disciples had basic knowledge that a messiah was coming. They were given intensive training as students of Jesus in the three years they were chosen followers.

As followers today we must be prepared to take on the authority given us as true disciples. To undertake a journey of discipleship we must study Jesus' teachings to the twelve, following the preparation process and the instructions they received. When Jesus sends out his disciples He not only tells them what to wear, but how to interact with the people they encountered. Scripture states that Jesus summoned the twelve to him and gave them power and authority over all demons and to cure diseases, and He sent them to proclaim the kingdom of God and to heal.

He said to them, "Take nothing for the journey, neither walking stick, nor sack, nor food, nor money, and let no one take a second tunic. Whatever house you enter, stay there and leave from there. And as for those who do not welcome you, when you leave that town, shake the dust from your feet in testimony against them." Then they set out and went from village to village proclaiming the good news and curing diseases everywhere.

They were to perform the same works that Jesus had shown them during his ministry and they were to completely rely upon God during this time (Luke 12:22-31).

Their transformation took place through study, hearing and exercising the power and authority of the Word of God. They were provided OJT (on the job training) that would lead to a greater relationship with God and complete reliance upon God. The training and instructions Jesus provided for the disciples of

His days on earth, would cross time and generational lines and become the foundation upon which discipleship stands today. It would be safe to say that the names have changed, but the task remains the same. The transformation of God's children into disciples equipped with the knowledge and purpose of discipleship actively evangelizing others for inclusion into the body of Christ–the church.

The most important and powerful tool of a disciple is the Word of God. Jesus illustrates the importance of understanding the Word of God in Mark 4:14-20.

'Then Jesus said to them, Don't you understand this parable? How then will you understand any parable? The farmer sows the word. Some people are like seed along the path, where the word is sown. As soon as they hear it, Satan comes and takes away the word that was sown in them. Others, like seed sown on rocky places, hear the word and at once receive it with joy. But since they have no root, they last only a short time. When trouble or persecution comes because of the word, they quickly fall away. Still others, like seed sown among thorns, hear the word; but the worries of this life, the deceitfulness of wealth and the desires for other things come in and choke the word, making it unfruitful. Others, like seed sown on good soil, hear the word, accept it, and produce a crop—some thirty, some

sixty, some a hundred times what was sown."

With discipleship, when the seed (The Word of God) is sown on good soil it is heard, accepted and produces a crop. In 2 Timothy 3: 16-17 the Apostle Paul writes, ***"All Scripture is God-breathed and is useful for teaching, rebuking, correcting and training in righteousness, so that the servant of God may be thoroughly equipped for every good work."***

In the Gospel of Matthew 28:18-20, Jesus gave His disciples one more command, ***"Then Jesus came to them and said, All authority in heaven and on earth has been given to me. Therefore go and make disciples of all nations, baptizing them in the name of the Father and of the Son and of The Holy Spirit, and teaching them to obey everything I have commanded you. And surely I am with you always, to the very end of the age."***

It is by His authority that we (believers) are commissioned to make disciples. Jesus has even given us the template (formula) for successful discipleship.

1. Go–out into the world.
2. Baptize–in the name of the Father and the Son and The Holy Spirit.
3. Teach–obedience to God.

4. And we are not doing this alone. Jesus is with us always to the very end of the age!

As we take a closer look at discipleship I ask you meditate on the scripture that brings God's great love for his children into focus for you. Open your eyes and ears to the reality that the events from Christ's conception to His ascension were not the end, but the beginning. The Bible is the testimony of God and His love for His creation. There is no greater love story than this. We, as the children of God, are admonished to walk in the way of love. In 1 Corinthians 13:4-8 we are given a beautiful and true definition of love. As the scriptures state: God is love. We can easily replace the word "love" in these scriptures with God. Love is patient, kind, does not envy, does not boast, not easily angered, keeps no record of wrong, does not delight in evil, rejoices in truth, protects, trusts, preserves, never fails. God is patient, kind, does not envy, does not boast, not easily angered, keeps no record of wrong, does not delight in evil, rejoices in truth, protects, trusts, preserves, never fail. How many of these attributes of love can you put your name in front of? It is for this love that disciples seek to bring others into the kingdom so that they too may know the love of God. Praise God for the sacrifice of Jesus. Elevate your discipleship, disciple, take it to the next level!

Ready to write?

Today's Date:

_____

_____

_____

_____

_____

_____

_____

_____

_____

_____

_____

_____

_____

_____

_____

2 WHAT IS THE MISSION OF A DISCIPLE?

Purpose:
To understand how Jesus equipped all disciples for the mission.

Hearing the Word:
Matthew 28:18-20
Then Jesus came to them and said, "All authority in heaven and on earth has been given to me. Therefore go and make disciples of all nations, baptizing them in the name of the Father and of the Son and of The Holy Spirit, and teaching them to obey everything I have commanded you. And surely I am with you always to the very end of the age."

Story:

Jesus left no doubt in the minds of His disciples as to where His authority in heaven and earth had come from. We understand the "all" in Jesus' statement to mean "every." *The American Heritage College Dictionary* defines the word "all" as the whole of one's resources or energy; everything one has. Wholly, completely, everyone, everything one has.

Authority, the second word, is defined as the power to enforce laws, exact obedience, command, determine or judge. It also means, "One that is invested with this power." The next phrase of utmost importance is, "has been given to Me" indicating that God has given Jesus a share in God's reign over creation. This is the mission of each disciple.

It is the authority given to Jesus that He uses to empower His disciples. The word "therefore" links the authority from God to Jesus then to humanity. Therefore, is defined as, "for that reason or cause, consequently or hence." Jesus delegated this authority to His disciples, therefore, they were acting on His authority to go and to make disciples of all nations. This delegated authority is the authority by which disciples of today are still commanded to carry out the work of discipleship.

To make disciples was only one command given to Jesus' disciples. Additional direction included:

1. Proclaiming the good news of the Gospel.
2. Curing the sick.
3. Cleansing the lepers.
4. Casting out demons.
5. Baptizing in the name of The Holy Spirit.

The English word "baptism" comes from the Greek verb that means, "to dip in water."

The most wonderful baptism took place at the Jordan River. It was there that John baptized Jesus and the voice of God was heard confirming Jesus as His son.

Matthew 3:16, 17 states:
"As soon as Jesus was baptized, he went up out of the water. At that moment heaven was opened, and he saw the Spirit of God descending lime a dove and lighting on him. And a voice from heaven said, "This is my Son, whom I love; with him I am well pleased." John preached and baptized in order to encourage people to repent of their sins, turn back to God, and be forgiven."

Do you remember your baptismal day? To whom had Jesus extended his authority to baptize you? Several people remember the exact date, time and place of their baptismal experience. And with great enthusiasm they often share with joy the events of that wondrous day.

Edna remembers being baptized in the local swimming pool. Only minutes following the baptism ceremony, everyone in her small, local town was enjoying the cool waters of the community swimming pool. For her the pool had been transformed into a holy place for certifying her belief in the triune God. Many years later she would share with her children, then her grandchildren how The Holy Spirit had come with her to the local pool.

Louis says his church had an elaborate baptismal pool. The water was warm, and his entire family had shown up for the event. He and all of his siblings had been baptized on the same day. Even his best friend, Evan, had made the decision for Christ on that day.

Christina was not baptized in a pool; her form of baptizing was called "pouring" where water was poured over her. Latisha says water was "sprinkled" over her when she was a 6-month-old newborn. By three different methods (dunking, pouring and sprinkling) each one was baptized unto the Father, Son and Holy Spirit.

One great epiphany is that the authority to baptize you was given to the person of God by God. Imagine…Jesus sent someone along the path that led them to baptizing you in His authority.

Jesus ended the scripture with this statement:
"And surely I am with you always to the very end of the age."

Jesus was not passing the work of discipleship on to His disciples because He told them, "I am with you always." Jesus is still actively taking part in the activities He has shared with His disciples. "And surely, He said I am with you, always to the end of the age": go therefore.

Ready to write?

Today's Date:

---

3 HOW DO I RELATE TO GOD AS A DISCIPLE?

Purpose:
To understand the expectation, attitude and accomplishments of the disciples' work in the mission field.

Hearing the Word:
John 13:15
"I have set you an example that you should do as I have done for you."

Story:

How often as parents do we say to our young ones, "do as I say not as I do." There are a greater number of times in life where we (especially church folk) will say, "you never know who is watching your actions." In this Scripture Jesus shows His divinity. He has set a higher standard as overseer for His disciples' teaching and care. The disciple is to relate to God as Jesus did. To see God as Father and provider of all godly things the disciple needs and desires. Jesus says:

"I have set you an example."

It is both indicative of a time in the present life and the future life of those who will carry on the ministry of Christ. Jesus has lived with His disciples for three years and says to them, *I have set you an example. In the three years of My ministry, teaching and life with you twelve I have been the example by which you shall live your future. Remember our days together and the trials and tribulations, events, healings, the people we have encountered, the miracles I have performed, the parables I have deciphered for you, the praying we have learned together, the evil we have triumphed over and how I have shown you through the Word and will of God to overcome. Remember my life...it is the example that will lead you in future days.*

"That you should do."

When faced with the world, remember how to handle a situation with prayer, humility and faith not in yourselves but in God My Father. Jesus was dependent upon God His Father for all things.

"As I have done for you."

In this last stanza Jesus is reminding the disciples

why He came to earth; to carry out the will of God for humanity's salvation.

Jesus introduced His disciples to every aspect of the five-fold ministry: pastor, teacher, evangelist, prophet, and apostle. He trained them in all aspects of ministry; preparing them for the work of God on.

Disciples must humbly submit themselves to serving God. Not only must they have the character of Jesus but must also look to God as Father.

Ready to write?

Today's Date:

_____

_____

_____

_____

_____

_____

_____

_____

_____

_____

_____

_____

_____

_____

_____

4 WHAT DOES MY DISCIPLESHIP COST ME?

Purpose:
To reflect that Christ instructions on discipleship still hold true today.

Hearing the Word:
Mark 1:18
"At Once they left their nets and followed him."

Matthew 10:37-39
"Anyone who loves their father or mother more than me is not worthy of me; anyone who loves their son or daughter more than me is not worthy of me. [39]Whoever finds their life shall loose it, and whoever loses there for life for my sake will find it."

Story:

There are several scriptural versions of Mark 1:18 that begin with the word immediately. This word alone does two things for the reader of the scripture. First, it speaks to the importance and timing of the statement. Immediately (Gk. *erthys*), which appears over forty times in this Gospel, is one of Mark's favorite words, (1:20-21, 23, 28-30, 42-43, 2:8, 12). It speeds the narrative up to an almost breathless pace. Here the "at once" also displays the immediacy as to which the disciples left their work and followed Jesus. They left everything behind and were obedient to his command to follow him. Obedience is defined as compliance with an order, request or law or submission to another's authority, and is central in describing the disciples' relationship with Jesus and their reaction to his (future) commands. There is an implied understanding on behalf of the disciples that they knew who Jesus was during this interaction because they did not hesitate or delay following his first command.

In Matthew 10:34-39 Jesus further defines His ministry for His disciples. He tells them that the mission they are about to undertake will affect family life. Family loyalty is subordinated and families are redefined not by birth (a critique of social hierarchy sustained by lineage and hereditary wealth) but by doing God's will. Love for Jesus is primary (10:37).

Jesus took twelve men as His disciples, and a following of many others (which included many women) and He conveyed to them the perfect love of 1 Corinthians 13:4. The love that Jesus shows us through his three-year interactions with His disciples (and the people) is patient, kind, does not envy nor boast and is not rude, self-seeking, angered, nor keeps account of wrong doings. The great love that Jesus shares is seen in His interactions with Peter. The disciple, who would deny Jesus (John 18:15-27) then restate his love for Jesus three times when Jesus asked him pointedly (John 21:15-17), "Simon son of John, do you love me more that these?" Three times Peter answered," Yes, you know that I love you." Finally Jesus said to Peter again, "Follow me." Our Scripture states:

Whoever finds their life shall loose it, and whoever loses there for life for my sake will find it. Peter would be both the literal and physical interpretation of this scripture, which relates to love and forgiveness. Jesus conversation with Peter is recorded as taking place before (the crucifixion) and after (the resurrection) the cross.

No earthly story can truly relate to the love that Jesus had for His disciples through the three years of teaching and growing them into discipleship. We are still learning from the interactions Jesus had with them and the ones He is having with us today. The tools and instructions that He gave them for success are still the ones we use today for discipleship.

Adam's story about how his friend Josh came to Christ is somewhat in alignment with this verse. Adam undertook a self-given task to save his buddy Josh and bring him into a relationship with Christ. Adam had been "saved since he was twelve and knew that having a healthy relationship with Jesus as his Lord and Savior would greatly improve Josh's expectation of life. Josh on the other hand knew Jesus. He too had grown up in the church. Around 11 years old Josh had begun to stray away from the church community and gotten in trouble with the local law enforcement agency on several occasions, even after spending three years of his life locked behind bars at the local penitentiary facility. Now Josh was trying to start anew. With the help of a few faithful friends, Josh was ready to return to "normal life."

Adam loved him enough to see beyond the day-to-day drama to want the best the future held for Josh so he invited him to church. Week after week Adam persisted with his invitations to get Josh to return to church. At first Josh brushed him off with a "someday" smile. Adam continued to tell Josh about the peace and joy he had in his walk with Christ. Josh found himself at odds with everyone who knew his past and was not willing to allow him the grace to have a future. Adam reminded Josh about Peter the disciple of Jesus. He told him about how Jesus had loved Peter back into the fold of His chosen disciples. Adam had learned about Jesus as the greatest teacher of discipleship. Jesus would be ready to take Josh into the church body and use his life story to bring in others with similar backgrounds. Jesus had written the guide on discipleship training and instruction. Adam envisioned that after intense Bible study to get acclimated in his own sonship, Josh to would hear the call of Jesus that Peter heard: do you love me?–feed my sheep. Adam also knew from experience that Josh would not lose his life on this journey; he was more sure that Josh would find his life in Jesus.

Ready to write?

Today's Date:

_____

_____

_____

_____

_____

_____

_____

_____

_____

_____

_____

_____

_____

_____

_____

_____

_____

5 WHAT ARE THE BENEFITS OF DISCIPLESHIP?

Purpose:
To lead an abundant life through obedience and faithfulness.

Hearing the Word:
Matthew 11:20
"...then Jesus began to denounce the towns in which most of his miracles had been performed, because they did not repent.

Story:

Early in Deuteronomy 30:18 God pronounced the sentence that would be invoked on those that were not obedient.

"If your heart turns away and you are not obedient and if you are drawn away to bow down

to their gods and worship them, I declare to you this day that you will certainly be destroyed. You will not live long in the land. You are crossing the Jordan to enter and possess."

This is the Old Testament Scripture that was delivered through Moses. Jesus in the New Testament is denouncing Korazin and Bethsaida, which were Jewish towns north of the Sea of Galilee.

The people of both towns were unrepentant. The punishment had been given to them by God through Moses was not being announced again by Jesus. Jesus began to denounce them, to publicly declare their wrong and evil ways and to bring them to repentance before they were punished for their behavior. Repentance (the feeling or to express sincere regret or remorse about their wrongdoing and sin) was the only way to avoid pending demise. He tells them it will be more bearable for Sodom on the Day of Judgment than for them.

God's command for obedience was easily defined in Deuteronomy 11.

"Now what I am commanding you today is not too difficult for you or beyond your reach."

Jesus gave an additional warning. There are consequences to disobedience. Parents often warn their children about the punishment associated with disobedience as a way of avoidance. Knowing the outcome of disobedience is supposed to deter offenders. For the Israelites the outcomes were life and prosperity or death and destruction. Jesus' warning was that the outcome was imminent if change was not seen.

On many occasions during my childhood Vacation Bible School days the "ruler of doom" was set to handle any and many acts of disobedience. Though not total annihilation, it posed a threat to every underhanded, outrageous, plot we could dream up. Standing before the class to recite The Beatitudes (Matthew5) or The 10 Commandments was a heart wrenching experience when the "ruler of doom" was used. Granted there are more severe life rules and regulations that, when broken, have dire consequences, but I never envision myself being involved at that level.

"For I command you today to love the Lord your God, to walk in obedience to him, and keep his commands, decrees and laws; then you will live and increase, and the Lord your God will bless you in the land you are entering to possess" (Deuteronomy 30:19.

Although an Old Testament command, Jesus compares disobedience across time spans. The outcomes have remained the same—death and destruction. Disciples are to take this message to those outside of the Body of Christ. Discipleship demands that the truth be shared with those who do not know, or don't realize the consequences of living life outside of The Church.

There are three Greek words used in the New Testament to denote repentance:

1. *Metamelomai*–used as change of mind, such as to produce regret or even remorse on account of sin, but not necessarily a change of heart.
2. *Metanoeo*–meaning to change one's mind and purpose, as the result of after knowledge.
3. *Metanoia*–used of true repentance, a change of mind and purpose and life, to which remission of sin is promised.

Evangelical repentance consists of:

1. A true sense of one's own guilt and sinfulness.
2. An apprehension of God's mercy in Christ.
3. An actual hatred of sin (Ps. 119:128, Job 42:5, 6; 2 Cor.7: 10) and tuning from it to God.
4. A persistent endeavor after a holy life in walking with God in the way of His commands.

Repentance comprehends, not only such a sense of sin, but also an apprehension of mercy, without which there can be no true repentance.

Psalm 51: 1-2:

Have mercy on me, O God, according to your unfailing love; according to your great compassion, blot out my transgressions, wash away all my iniquity, and, cleanse me from my sin.

Psalm 130:4:

But with you there is forgiveness, so that we can, with reverence, serve you.

Repentance and transforming one's life through the redemptive work of Jesus Christ is the only way to avoid the outcomes of disobedience on both a personal and national level is through Jesus Christ. God has given us the clear to choose when situations arise in which, we believe, we must make a decision for positive or negative activity (physical or mental). No one who is born of God will continue to sin, because God's seed remains in them; they cannot go on sinning because they have been born of God. The Scriptures make up the main part of the disciples' tools and become the foundation of discipleship. They are God's breath and good for training. In this situation John 3:36 (NIV), clearly states: "Whoever believes in the Son has eternal life, but whoever rejects the Son will not see life for God's wrath remains on them." The path for disciples that leads others to God flows through knowledgeable and Christ-based discipleship.

Ready to write?

Today's Date:

_____

_____

_____

_____

_____

_____

_____

_____

_____

_____

_____

_____

6 WHAT DID JESUS DO FOR THE DISCIPLES?

Purpose:
To understand the directive Jesus gave to his disciples and the utmost importance it is for today's dedicated disciples.

Hearing the Word:
2 Corinthians 5:15
And he died for all, that those who live should no longer live for themselves but for him who died for them and was raised again.

Matthew 4:19
"Come, follow me," Jesus said, "and I will send you out to fish for people."

Story:

Jesus' purpose was to be the last sacrifice for human sinners and to overcome death, providing eternal life to God's human creation. God made the heavens and the earth and all that dwell within them. He redeemed humanity from the sin the first Adam and Eve committed in the Garden of Eden through the works of Jesus Christ, God's only begotten son, who was born of The Holy Spirit, who fulfilled the law and the prophets. God, the creator of all things created, loved us so much that he gave His only begotten son, that we who believe in Him would receive eternal life. We are alive in Jesus. Paul explains the transition from death to eternal life in his epistle to the Romans (6:19-23 NIV) as follows:

I am using an example from everyday life because of your human limitations. Just as you used to offer yourselves as slaves to impurity and to ever-increasing wickedness, so now offer yourselves as slaves to righteousness leading to holiness. When you were slaves to sin, you were free from the control of righteousness. What benefit did you reap at that time from the things you are now ashamed of? Those things result in death! But now that you have been set free from sin and have become slaves of God, the benefit you reap leads to holiness, and the result is eternal life. For the wages of sin is death, but the gift of God is eternal life in Christ Jesus our Lord.

Please note verse 23b in the scripture above. It speaks of "the gift" of God as eternal life in Christ Jesus!! Jesus helped many lost find the way to salvation. Jesus saved us from our sins. Today we say that He paid the ransom that provided for our salvation and therefore our eternal life which we obtain through our belief in Him and His redemptive work.

Matthew 4:19

"Come follow me, Jesus said, "and I will send you out to fish for people."

Jesus called to himself twelve disciples. *Easton's Bible Dictionary* defines disciple as a scholar, principally applied to the followers of Christ. A disciple of Christ is one who:

1. Believed His doctrine,
2. Rests on His sacrifice,
3. Imbibed His spirit and
4. Imitated His example (Matthew 10:24; Luke 14:26, 27, 33; John 6:69).

Jesus' disciples give us the best view of the purpose and work of disciples (discipleship) from their work to their expectation of those who would follow the work of Jesus.

Mark 3:14-15 states, "He appointed twelve that they might be with Him and that He might send them out to preach and to have authority to drive out demons."

Peter wrote in 1 Peter 2:21 of those who were disciples,

"To this you were called, because Christ suffered for you, leaving you an example, that you should follow in his steps."

Matthew tells us that there will be true and false disciples in Matthew 7:21-23.

"Not everyone who says to me, 'Lord, Lord,' will enter the kingdom of heaven, but only the one who does the will of my Father who is in heaven. Many will say to me on that day, 'Lord, Lord, did we not prophesy in your name and in your name drive out demons and in your name perform many miracles?' Then I will tell them plainly, 'I never knew you. Away from me, you evildoers!'

Jesus said of those who wanted to follow Him that they "must deny themselves and take up their cross and follow me" as recorded in Mark 8:34.

Philippians 2:6-7 records the best description of the purpose of a disciple as it speaks of the servant attitude Jesus Christ,

"Who, being in very nature God, did not consider equality with God something to be used to his

own advantage; rather, he made himself nothing by taking the very nature of a servant, being made in human likeness."

Webster's Dictionary defines servanthood as the noun form of servant. The definition given to servant is a devoted and helpful follower or supporter.

In Matthew 28:19 we servants of God are directed to imitate Jesus and to make disciples of all nations, baptizing them in the name of the Father and the Son and of The Holy Spirit. Teaching them the ways and will of God as we have learned them from the life of Christ.

All believers easily understand the scripture in 2 Corinthians. It was Jesus who was the last sacrificial offering. We preach about the Son of God, whom God gave to redeem the world's sin. Of His death Paul said, "For Christ's love compels us, because we are convinced that one died for all, and therefore all died." His life is the foundational stone of discipleship and a life in Christ.

There are many books (including this one) and other media that use the Scriptures to help us understand the roll of the disciple in the world today. We watch videos, read books, yet the greatest journal remains The Holy Bible, which outlines the life of Jesus. Our church finds it imperative that we continue to follow the works of Christ in making disciples. It is a global task of great importance to all humanity. Jesus instructed the disciples in Mark (10:14) and in Luke (10:11) how to handle global discipleship work noting that there are those who will not be receptive. However, the work of spreading the Gospel must continue. Jesus sent out his seventy-two disciples with these specific instructions found in Luke 10:9: Heal the sick who are there and tell them, 'The kingdom of God has come near to you.'

We continue to "fish for people as Jesus directed his disciples. A directive I have shared with my church disciples and ambassadors. Our church continues to seek new ways to introduce people to God and get them involved in the work going on in The Body. October is our month for Friends and Family Day. All current disciples invite friends and family to worship with us. This year we took this event to a new level by inviting the city community to join us. We invited the local police department, military personnel and local non-profit groups to join us for services, as well as, events such as our annual church picnic outing. We provided financial support to local youth groups and proudly presented all group representatives with plaques of appreciation for the services they provide to our community.

We were happy with the response we received, and look forward to our spring Youth Explosion and Conference Leadership Training School held during the early summer months.

Multitudes of disciples are going out today with the same instructions, message and knowledge that Jesus gave His followers when He told them, "The harvest is plentiful, but the workers are few. Ask the Lord of the harvest, therefore, to send out workers into his harvest field. Go! I am sending you out like lambs among wolves" (Luke 10: 2-3).

Ready to write?

Dr. Amanda Goodson

Today's Date:

_____

_____

_____

_____

_____

_____

_____

_____

_____

_____

_____

_____

_____

_____

_____

7 THE PROPER DESIRE OF A DISCIPLE

Purpose:

To use every tool available to bring others into a righteous relationship with God.

Hearing the Word:
Philippians 2:5
"In your relationships with one another, have the same mindset as Christ Jesus."

Jesus spent time training His disciples and getting to love and to know them. In John 13:34 Jesus said to them, "A new command I give you; Love one another. As I have loved you, so you must love one another." Then he added, "By this everyone will know that you are my disciples, if you love one another. As disciples of today we understand this to mean that we must love each other (fellow believers)

43

and all humanity. We are given a definition of love in 1 Corinthians 13 that speaks to our spiritual love for one another. We see the importance of relationships from the beginning of creation. Adam longed for a helpmate so God created Eve. Man is a relational creature. Webster defines relational as:

1. Of or relating to kinship
2. Characterized or constituted by relations
3. Having the function chiefly of indicating a relation of syntax.

The word "relationships" refers to the way in which two or more concepts, objects or people are connected. In Exodus 25:8, God gave Moses this command for the Israelites:

"Then have them make a sanctuary for me, and I will dwell among them."

In 2 Corinthians 6 verses 16 and 18 the Apostle Paul speaks against relationships between believers (God's temple) and unbelievers (idol worshipers). More importantly he speaks of believers as the temple of the living God. He writes:

As God has said: "I will live with them and walk among them, and I will be their God, and they will be my people." And, "I will be a Father to you, and you will be my sons and daughters, says the Lord Almighty."

Above Paul speaks to the relationship between God and man (those of us who are believers). The proper desire for a disciple is to use every tool available to him to bring others into a righteous relationship with God. As Jesus has stated, His work was to seek and save that which was lost. Having the mindset of Jesus means focusing on the work that God has called each of us to through discipleship. Jesus focused on accomplishing the work He was sent into the world to do. His attitude was one of humility and determination to complete His work. God was at the central focus of all that Jesus did during His ministry. Jesus prayed often. He was focused on accomplishing the purpose of God for His life. He spoke these very powerful words which gave great clarity to his purpose on earth when He said to God, "not my will but your will be done."

Story:

We often notice during times of trial that we need God to be with us. Anthony believed his climb up the corporate ladder was due to his outstanding talent. He had paid his dues educationally when he strove across the stage to collect accolades for getting his PhD. He had made it to the big time, for everything, life, love and career began to align to his expectations of success. He had often noted that he could make his way without support from anyone. Life was harsh for others but not for him because

Anthony knew how to pull himself up by his bootstraps and move along the lines of success. He had everything that he needed. When he took time to look around he noticed that there were so many in lack. This tugged at his heart. He found himself often asking the question of why so many were in need.

One day on the way home Anthony encountered an old friend, a high school buddy who looked quite old for his young years. Anthony wanted to help but felt the few dollars he could give was not enough. His friend invited him to join him for lunch. He was on his way to a church that had an awesome food line. Anthony went along and found himself helping serve others. The next week he went back to help serve, and the next and on his third visit he joined the group and became a regular participant often giving up his nights to help out.

He found himself going to church on Sunday mornings and helping out there. More and more Anthony began to understand that his journey had not been by his own might alone. Finally he dedicated his life to Christ; being reborn he began to reexamine his life goals. He loved his new life without the constant stress and helping others was exciting. Anthony had begun a new walk with Christ. He made a decision to be a committed follower of Jesus. He knew that the proper desire of a true disciple is to enable others to become disciples. Spreading the Gospel of Jesus Christ to all nations seemed a reasonable task to undertake. With help of his pastor and friends he would discover that a great journey lay ahead.

Ready to write?

Today's Date:

8 WHAT IS THE CALL OF A DISCIPLE?

Purpose:
To bring the illuminated word of God into dark paces and show non-believers the way to Christ.

Hearing the Word:
Matthew 5:14–16
"You are the light of the world. A town built on a hill cannot be hidden. Neither do people light a lamp and put it under a bowl. Instead they put it on its stand, and it gives light to everyone in the house. In the same way, let your light shine before others; that they may see your good deeds and glorify your Father in heaven."

1 Peter 2:21

"To this you were called, because Christ suffered for you, leaving you an example, that you should

follow in his steps.

1 Peter 2:9
"But you are a chosen people, a royal priesthood, a holy nation, God's special possession, that you may declare the praises of him who called you out of darkness into his wonderful light."

Story:

As a disciple of God your light should shine amongst all humanity regardless of your personal situations. A disciple of Jesus brings light into dark situations and every house. The light of the disciple should look like the light of Jesus. A description of Jesus would include words such as humble and bold. Disciples are to bring the illuminated Word of God into those dark paces and show non-believers the way to Christ.

The Hebrew words *ahal*, or, *halal*, are all translated "shine." In a direct and literal sense the word "shine" is used of the heavenly bodies, or of candles and fire (Job 18:5; 25:5). The New Testament words *astrapto*, *augazo*, *lampo* and *phaino* are also translated "shine." Thus, literally it is said of the lightning that it shines (Matthew 24:27, KJV; Luke 17:24); the word is tropically applied to the life of faith or to men prominent in the kingdom of God (Matthew 5:16; John 5:35; 2 Corinthians 4:6; Philippians 2:15; 2 Peter 1:19); to the glory of God (Luke 2:9); to angelic appearances (Luke 24:4; Acts 12:7).

LaKeisha thought to herself that the hard times would be short times. She would soon be back to work and everything would begin to flow again for her and her children. Sometimes she sat in awe of how strong they were and proudly smiled when she saw her young son trying to step up and take care of his older sisters. The sadness found its way back into her heart as she would soon have to tell her son that she could not afford the basketball camp he was attending. It was his only request for the season. He knew if he could continue to get the coach's attention then the scholarship offer was his, guaranteed. He had only three weeks to go before the decision would be made as to whether or not the school would make him an offer. It was the only way his family could afford to send him to a better school.

Things had been different when Dad was around. It was evident that harder times were ahead once dad had left the family. With dad they were broke, but without him they were even more broke. Dad left but the love didn't leave. They still had each other and would find a way to make it work for their good.

Yep, LaKeisha nodded, agreeing with her thoughts. God had promised to take what was meant for their detriment and change it around for their good. God knew her heart and her family, smiling she said, "this too shall pass." She would not be able to keep him in the practice program. She knew what this meant to him and his future.

Her first priority was to change everyone's fate by finding a job. She put on her big heavy coat for added protection from the snow, and headed out the door to look for work, thinking surely, someone needed her job skills. As she walked she prayed a prayer of hope. Her conversation with God always gave her hope that just around the corner was the answer to all her needs; she only had to figure which corner. She prayed past the local drug store, prayed past the local restaurant, prayed past the car dealership and entered the local mart to get warm.

Once inside she noticed how busy everyone was, and she missed that energy that came from working. She sat down in the daily area to rest for a moment. She smiled her best, tired, cold and hungry smile at the kid across the table from her. He looked to be more down in spirit than she was so she said hello and asked if he was ok. He nodded weakly. She offered to buy him a drink (which she could not afford) and was secretly happy when he said no thank you. They sat in silence then she asked him if there was something she could do to cheer up his day. "No, thank you," he said and they once again sat in silence.

Finally she got up to continue her journey. She said to her co-sitting friend, "I pray your day will get better."

"Thank you," he nodded, "and yours also."

"Well, she said, if I find a job up the road, it will."

"What kind of job are you looking for?" he asked.

She smiled her best stop asking questions smile and responded, "Right now I would take any job I can find. This is my desperation search. I am not too particular right now; I know I will find something today."

"You know anything about management he asked? Any skills working with people, supervising people," he asked, "Seriously?" She quoted all the information on her résumé to him. She had memorized it, and practiced it quite often today, she thought, and then asked, him, "Why…do you know someone with a job opening?

"Me," he said. "I am the manager here and I am looking for an assistant manager, are you interested?" Then he quoted all the required skills necessary to do the job. He knew them well because he had held the position for three years himself. "Around here we work very long hours, but the pay is good."

He smiled, and she smiled. When LaKeisha tells the story she says, "On that day, God smiled." The walk home was pleasant and she prayed a thankful prayer.

Ready to write?

Today's Date:

_____

_____

_____

_____

_____

_____

_____

_____

_____

_____

_____

_____

_____

9 HOW DOES JESUS SERVE HIS DISCIPLES?

Purpose:
To prepare humanity for discipleship.

Hearing the Word:
John 13:12-14
When he had finished washing their feet; he put on his clothes and returned to his place. "Do you understand what I have done for you?" he asked them. [13] "You call me 'Teacher' and 'Lord' and rightly so, for that is what I am. [14] Now that I, your Lord and Teacher, have washed your feet, you also should wash one another's feet."

Story:

There is no argument about the humility that Jesus

showed in washing the feet of His disciples. The feet were the mode of transportation during that time; taking care of them was of utmost importance. Washing required kneeling or bowing down at the foot of the person to wash away the dirt and grim gathered during the day's toils.

Jesus knew that the Father had put all things under His power and that He had come from God and was returning to God. He also knew that the time had come when He would be separated from His disciples. The greatest lesson that He would teach them required that He be separated from them physically so that He could be with them (and all humanity) spiritually.

It was the precursory event to His last days as a physical person on this earth. This would be His last physical touch of each of the disciples. His body would be laid to rest in a tomb that belonged to another for as in life He had not a resting place of his own; no place to rest in life and no place to rest in death.

Just as life could not dictate His daily events, or restrain His coming and going, in and out amongst the people He loved and served; neither could death, Hades or Sheol restrain the Son of God. As He had knelt before His Father God, in prayer, Jesus now knelt before man in love. In this moment Jesus, the King of Kings and Lord of Lords, knelt before man to again teach of love, obedience, servitude and humility.

Think on this for a moment and envision what happened from the moment of preparation to the washing of each disciple's feet.

- The meal was being served when Jesus got up—servants were not to eat first, but only after everyone else had been filled. Jesus in serving His disciples as they had served Him, would elevate them from servants to friends.
- Just as Adam had sought to cover his nakedness from God in Eden to hide his sin, Jesus removed his outer clothing, for in Him was knowledge and wisdom.
- His first step was to wrap himself with a towel, just as the first piece of armor of God to put on is the loin cloth of truth.

He poured water in a basin and washed the feet of ones who would abandon Him, one who would deny him and one who would betray him. This water differed from the water He had shared with the Samaritan woman, through whom He still tells all humanity about the power of living water. Had He reflected on His three years, or so, He would have an awesome list of accomplishments:

- He taught fishermen to fish for men.
- He showed humanity that true love is of God.

- He taught humanity the importance of submission to God.
- He taught humanity how to pray to the God that created them.
- He taught humanity the power of God to rule over death.
- He taught humanity obedience to God.
- He taught humanity about the healing power of God.
- He taught humanity that grace is of God.
- He taught humanity that God rules over demons and disease.
- In the days ahead, all humanity would come to know that salvation is of God.

This list is alive and growing. Please feel free to add your input to it.

Throughout the three years with His disciples He equipped them with the tools to serve humanity with integrity, honesty and humility. He equipped them with the knowledge to serve God in spirit and in truth. He told them the secret of coming before God is to come as a child of God. As Jesus would transfigure before them, gifting humanity with another Helper, The Holy Spirit, the disciples too would transform from students to teachers, preachers, prophets, evangelists and helpers going from discipleship to apostleship.

Joy approached her calling with grace and love for

she knew that God himself was pleased with the work she was doing. Her area of humility was talked about all throughout The Bible. She shared Jesus' heart for service. She never envisioned that someday she would wash someone's feet, but she knew in her own way she would enjoy teaching others to pray.

When asked what her calling was, she proudly proclaimed, I am a servant. This service was not limited to any specific group of people, wherever she could help, there she was, doing just that. Joy did notice that the more she was willing to serve others the more she was given to do. Every once in a while someone would come along side to help Joy with her tasks, and on occasion someone came along to take over a task. She never fretted about it for she knew if they did not like it she would get it back.

As Joy grew in God she could see The Spirit at work all around her. Her desire to study and share the word of God with others led her along a path toward ministry. She did not give it much thought for it was right and natural to her. The trials that came along sent her searching for God in all things. Her life took unexpected twists and turns, but Joy held on to Jesus and the promises of God. What she discovered was God would not complain about her or her gifts. God would supply her needs for health and prosperity.

Joy knew that God loved her and she wanted to

share that love with others, but it was sometimes difficult for people to give and receive. Regardless of those around her, Joy was adamant about living the life that she preached.

Look around you and find the joy in your life. Thank God!

Ready to write?

Today's Date:

_____

_____

_____

_____

_____

_____

_____

_____

_____

_____

_____

10 WHAT DOES THE HOLY SPIRIT DO FOR DISCIPLES?

Purpose:
To be our Advocate providing strength and guidance.

Hearing the Word:
John 14:26
"But the Advocate, The Holy Spirit, whom the Father will send in my name, will teach you all things and will remind you of everything I have said to you."

Story:

An Advocate is one who pleads for another's cause, who helps another by defending or comforting him. It is a name given by Christ three times to the Holy

61

Ghost (John 14:16; 15:26; 16:7, where the Greek word is rendered "Comforter," q.v.). It is applied to Christ in
1 John 2:1, where the same Greek word is rendered "Advocate." It also means to teach or to show or explain to (someone) how to do something; instruct. In our Scripture, Jesus also tells His disciples that the advocate will also remind them of everything He said. To remind means to cause (someone) to remember someone or something; to bring something, especially a commitment or necessary course of action, to the attention of (someone).

When we think about moments when we were reminded of something we said there is often a child involved in the reminding. Children have a pointed way of reminding their parents of important promises or events. Most often the reminding is spurred on due to the forgetful mind.

Danielle tells a story of how it became her job to remind her parents to pick her up from daycare each day. This reminding was spurred on when they both forgot to carry out this complex task one evening. Both had made it home. Her older sister had come home with a friend after her volley ball game, and helped prepare the evening meal. As the family sat down to eat they noticed that Danielle was not home. They called the school principal, but no one answered the phone. There was no answer when they called the school daycare center. So they rushed to the school praying that their youngest daughter was not harmed. The school was locked and secure. After the principal answered their frantic call she too rushed over to the school. There was one lone light shining from the daycare center. When they entered the play area, there sat Danielle with one of the attendants who was not much older than Danielle. The attendant looked up and smiled and said you arrived just in time, "I called my mom and she is on her way to get us. I was told by the supervisor that you would pay me $15.00 an hour to stay with Danielle, so I decided to wait as long as I could," she said.

The principal advocated for the student attendant. She felt that we should pay both the regular fee for use of the school and the $15 per hour fee to the student.

No, the money for the four hour extended stay was not the reminder in this situation. Danielle brought it to their attention often reminding them over the years about the time they totally forgot to pick her up from school.

John 3:5-7

Jesus answered, very truly I tell you, no one can enter the kingdom of God unless they are born of water and the spirit. Flesh gives birth to flesh, but the Spirit gives birth to spirit. [7] You should not be surprised at my saying, 'You must be born again.'

Jesus called The Holy Spirit "another Helper" as He, Himself was the first. Jesus was willing to give Himself as a living sacrifice for all humanity.

In order to enter the kingdom of God we must be reborn of The Spirit. The Spirit bears witness with our spirit that we are children of God and if children, then heirs of God and joint heirs with Christ. The Holy Spirit represents the presence of God at work in the world. Jesus told the disciples that they would be baptized with The Holy Spirit (Acts 1:3-5) and that The Spirit would give them the power to be Jesus' witnesses "to the ends of the earth" (Acts 1:8). On the day of Pentecost, The Spirit came to the disciples (Acts 2:1-12). Acts shows us the many ways The Holy Spirit guided and strengthened the disciples as they moved forward to tell of the good news of Christ to other people (Acts 4:8,31; 6:3-5; 8:29, 13:2-12, 20:22-28). In Romans 8:1-17, Paul tells us it is The Holy Spirit who sets free God's new people and who changes their lives so that they can have peace and be obedient to God. The Spirit gives them the ability to understand God's will, to live together in love, to carry out different types of work within the church (1 Corinthians 12-14). In both Romans 8:9-13 and Galatians 5:22-23, The Spirit produces within us the love and the lifestyle that God wants for His people.

In John16 Jesus outlines the following that The Holy Spirit will do for His disciples:

- Convict the world of guilt in regard to sin and righteousness and judgment.
- Guide in all truth.
- Tell them what is to come.
- Bring glory to Jesus by taking from Him and making it known to the disciples.

Ready to write?

Dr. Amanda Goodson

Today's Date:

_____

_____

_____

_____

_____

_____

_____

_____

_____

_____

_____

_____

_____

_____

_____

_____

11 WHAT IS THE LOVE OF A FRUITFUL DISCIPLE?

Purpose:
To continue the work that Jesus began.

Hearing the Word:
John 15:9-14
"As the Father has loved me, so have I loved you. Now remain in my love. If you keep my commands, you will remain in my love, just as I have kept my Father's commands and remain in his love. I have told you this so that my joy may be in you and that your joy may be complete. My command is this: Love each other as I have loved you. Greater love has no one than this: to lay down one's life for one's friends. You are my friends if you do what I command."

Story:

We have talked extensively to this point about Jesus as the great example of discipleship. He taught the disciples by example. Jesus showed them and the world that they are capable of following His example. Everything He accomplished could then be completed through them. Jesus said, "My true disciples produce much fruit. This brings great glory to my Father" (John 15:8 NIV). Jesus also said, "By their fruits you will know them" (Matthew 7:20 NIV).

In my nine years as pastor of my church I have delivered several messages on Galatians 5:22-23 about the fruit of the Spirit. This Scripture states, "But the fruit of The Spirit is love, joy, peace, longsuffering, kindness, goodness, faithfulness, gentleness, self-control." As ambassadors and disciples of God these fruits are standard and identifiable in our character.

Like fruit farmers, we too are fruit producers. Our character should mimic the humble character of Christ. We are whole when this character is standard in our lives. We should not change when our situations change. We should love all and love all the time. Your fruit should shine in the darkest situations. You should never put Jesus on the curb while you conduct business according to the ways of the world. You should never display "spoiled fruit" characteristics. Spoiled fruit or anti-fruit displays negative characteristics. I tell my congregation of a time when I would decide to take care of a situation instead of praying through it. I would leave Jesus safe on the curb while I handled the situation at hand. Then, I would return and pick Him (my good fruit characteristics) up when I had finished. Those were my childish ways of handling the world. Now that I have put those away the good fruit of The Spirit is who I have become. Others should be able to identify your character by the positive fruit of the Spirit.

The first love of a fruitful disciple is to continue the work that Jesus began. The Scripture in several biblical books speaks to the production of positive fruit. Matthew 13:23 is a statement of our capability to produce the endless fruit. It states, "But the seed falling on good soil refers to someone who hears The Word and understands it. This is the one who produces a crop, yielding a hundred, sixty or thirty times what was sown."

The harvest of discipleship is the production of fruit producing disciples. Jesus said," As the Father has loved me, so have I loved you. Now remain in my love. If you keep my commands, you will remain in my love, just as I have kept my Father's commands and remain in his love. I have told you this so that my joy may be in you and that your joy may be complete." Love is very important in our life walk. Love is the greatest fruit one can produce.

Jesus said, "Greater love has no one than this: to lay down one's life for one's friends. You are my friends if you do what I command." Jesus proved His love for us when he gave His life that we may have eternal life. He is the only one who bore a cross for our sins. He is our friend; we should keep His commands.

Ready to write?

Today's Date:

_____

_____

_____

_____

_____

_____

_____

_____

_____

_____

_____

12 HOW DOES THE HOLY SPIRIT GUIDE DISCIPLES?

Purpose:
Trust the Spirit of truth in every area of your life.

Hearing the Word:
John 16:13
"But when he, the Spirit of truth, comes, he will guide you into all the truth. He will not speak on his own; he will speak only what he hears, and he will tell you what is yet to come."

1 Corinthians 2:13
"This is what we speak, not in words taught us by human wisdom but in words taught by the Spirit, explaining spiritual realities with Spirit-taught words."
Story:

The role of The Holy Spirit in discipleship is the same as the role of The Holy Spirit in all believers' lives. The Holy Spirit is the third person of the Trinity. Although He is mentioned in Scripture the day of Pentecost remains a remarkable point in which the promised Holy Spirit descended and was received by over 3000 people.

The Scripture outlines the work of The Holy Spirit for the disciple. The list below is by no means complete, but a soft look at a few selected from The Bible.

1) John 16:14:
   a) Guide in all truth
   b) Speak only what He hears
   c) Will tell you what is yet to come
   d) Will glorify Jesus
   e) Will teach you all things
   f) Will bring to your remembrance what Jesus said

2) 1 Corinthians:
   a) Distribution of Spiritual Gifts

3) John 14:16:
   a) Comforts

4) Ephesians 1:13; 4:30:
   a) Seal of believers to the day of redemption

b) Council

5) Acts 1:8:
   a) Baptism, "in fire or power" as spoken by Jesus

The first love of a fruitful disciple is to continue the work that Jesus began. These are but a few of the gifts of The Holy Spirit.

Jesus said he would leave "another helper" indicating that He (Jesus) was the first. Speaking in tongues is one of the gifts of The Holy Spirit. 1 Corinthians 12:4-10 states, " Now, there are varieties of gifts, but the same Spirit...to each is given the manifestation of The Spirit for the common good. For to one is given through The Spirit the utterance of wisdom, and to another the utterance of knowledge according to the same Spirit, to another faith by the same Spirit, to another gifts of healing by the one Spirit, to another the working of miracles, to another prophecy, to another the ability to distinguish between spirits, to another various kinds of tongues, to another the interpretation of tongues."

The Great Commission was the last recorded instruction given by Jesus to the disciples. Go therefore and make disciples of all nations. The Holy Spirit is one-third of the Holy Trinity yet also has His own characteristics. He has intellect, emotion and a will. He performs miracles, convinces and restrains;

He commands and directs people. He can be prayed to and asked to intercede on a person's behalf, and He also gives believers gifts. Some of these gifts include love, joy, peace, kindness, goodness and self-control. This list of gifts is known as the fruits of the spirit and are found in Galatians 5:22-23.

Ready to write?

Today's Date:

_____

_____

_____

_____

_____

_____

_____

_____

_____

_____

13 WHAT IS THE ELEVATION OF A DISCIPLE?

Purpose:
To be thoroughly equipped for every good work.

Hearing the Word:
Ephesians 1:3-17
"Praise be to the God and Father of our Lord Jesus Christ, who has blessed us in the heavenly realms with every spiritual blessing in Christ. For he chose us in him before the creation of the world to be holy and blameless in his sight. In love he predestined us for adoption to sonship through Jesus Christ, in accordance with his pleasure and will—to the praise of his glorious grace, which he has freely given us in the One he loves. In him we have redemption through his

blood, the forgiveness of sins, in accordance with the riches of God's grace that he lavished on us. With all wisdom and understanding, he made known to us the mystery of his will according to his good pleasure, which he purposed in Christ, to be put into effect when the times reach their fulfillment—to bring unity to all things in heaven and on earth under Christ.

In him we were also chosen, having been predestined according to the plan of him who works out everything in conformity with the purpose of his will, in order that we, who were the first to put our hope in Christ, might be for the praise of his glory. And you also were included in Christ when you heard the message of truth, the gospel of your salvation. When you believed, you were marked in him with a seal, the promised Holy Spirit, who is a deposit guaranteeing our inheritance until the redemption of those who are God's possession—to the praise of his glory.

For this reason, ever since I heard about your faith in the Lord Jesus and your love for all God's people, [16] I have not stopped giving thanks for you, remembering you in my prayers. I keep asking that the God of our Lord Jesus Christ, the glorious Father, may give you the Spirit of wisdom and revelation, so that you may know him better."

Story:

The section of Scriptures outlined above (Ephesians 1:3-17) written by the Apostle Paul contain his greetings, blessings and prayers. Paul was elected to take the Gospel News to the Gentile people. He wrote the letter to the saints in Ephesus, the faithful in Christ Jesus. The first elevation of a disciple is to believe in God and that Jesus the Son of God carried out the redemptive works of the cross. Christ still rules both heaven and earth. The disciple must recognize that he has been redeemed through the washing of the blood of Jesus and received forgiveness of sins, in accordance with the riches of God's grace. This is secondary to the belief that God created all things that are in heaven and on earth and the fall of man resulting from his encounters with the prince of darkness in the garden.

Spiritual blessings are given to the disciple and include forgiveness, wisdom and revelation, faith and the special gifts that are used to serve God. As in Jeremiah 1:5 the disciple must accept the realization that he was chosen before the foundation of the world to do the work to which he has been called and equipped by God. In the quest to follow Jesus' instruction to make disciples of all nations through learned discipleship (taught by Jesus to his chosen twelve) the disciple must know that God is not a respecter of persons and the order is given to make disciples of all nations and all people. It is imperative that the elevated disciple knows God's Word.

All Scripture is God-breathed and is useful for teaching, rebuking, correcting and training in righteousness, so that the servant of God may be thoroughly equipped for every good work (Timothy 3:16-17).

Disciples are to be the light that is never hidden but continuously guides others to God. Always cognizant of their lives and their lifestyles must be in alignment with God's Word and leads others to Christ. Elevation becomes the knowing and doing of God's will to save the lost unto salvation.

Most disciples have a story (a witness) to share about the works of God in their lives. Paul's story about his conversion from prosecutor to apostle is one of the most awesome witness stories in the bible.

Most revolve around a miraculous event that occurred in one's life. George considered himself an ordinary guy with a heart for God. He never wanted to be an active church going, tithing, holy, Sunday school teaching, prayer warrior, participating, praise loving worshiper. George spent one hour every Sunday–and only on Sunday–in church. He felt he had done his part. After service George had made a pact with himself that the rest of the day and the rest of his week was his to do as he pleased. He would spend his time doing the things he liked to do. Most often, he would go to the bookstore to read his Bible in quiet. He enjoyed reading and often found himself talking to God about the events of his life. God could give George a better explanation about all the things he had gone through; especially those that he thought, at the time they occurred, he would not survive. He felt close to God. He learned more that way–when he was alone. Every now and then George would share an event from his life story with others but only if he felt it was helpful to them. As he grew in knowledge about Christ, George felt good talking with others about the power of Jesus and the love of God. One day when he was deep in reflective thought reviewing his life, George thought he heard God say that it was time for him to give more of himself to ministry. He smiled and shook his head, it is amazing what the mind thinks it hears when contemplating the possibilities of an all-powerful God. George smiled again when the small voice called to him again and said, "Come walk with Me; I will make you fisher of men." *Wow*, George thought, *what a great cup of tea!*

Ready to write?

Dr. Amanda Goodson

Today's Date:

_____

_____

_____

_____

_____

_____

_____

_____

_____

_____

_____

_____

_____

_____

14 HOW IS A DISCIPLE STRENGTHENED?

Purpose:
To be rooted and grounded in prayer.

Hearing the Word:
Ephesians 3:16-18
"I pray that out of his glorious riches he may strengthen you with power through his Spirit in your inner being, so that Christ may dwell in your hearts through faith. And I pray that you, being rooted and established in love, may have power, together with all the Lord's holy people, to grasp how wide and long and high and deep is the love of Christ..."

Story:

As Paul prayed for the uplifting and well-being of the Ephesians, this Scripture applies to the whole Body of Christ that it may be strengthened (made stronger) through growth and love so that Christ my dwell in the hearts of the faithful. That the love of God for all humanity on which our salvation was established have power with all believers to know that this love exceed anything definable by man. For God, having given His only begotten Son for our redemption, love and strength as believers in all that He has created, has taken love to a standard far beyond anything man can conceive.

Prayer is the most powerful tool in the universe because it allows us to communicate with God. There is no condition or occasion which the praying person cannot share with God, if they are believers in God. Getting a prayer through to God is a matter of the heart of the warrior.

Kathleen prayed often that God would heal many people of those ailments or requirements they shared with her. She was the go-to prayer warrior who everyone thought could get a prayer through to God. She prayed for healing and prosperity, and freedom, and transformation, for many a saint. Her words were eloquent and prayers long. She wondered how effective they were. They were from the heart and sincere but she herself had not had a situation that involved her own needs. Until now; as she lay weak and empty from hours spent in prayer to God to heal her husband. He had been strong throughout his illness and took it well when the doctors said that there was nothing more they could do. Kathleen heard the words, but knew that all had not been placed before God. Months, maybe weeks were the words out of the doctor's mouth. Her thoughts were centered on God and she heard no more than that. "God," she whispered, "They are not the maker and ruler over my life. I belong to you. We worship you as creator and Lord Jesus whose blood covers and cleanses us. Holy Spirit, I rebuke the words being spoken now, in the name of Jesus and bind them to the river of fire where they cannot fester or grow but will be held captive until the day of Jesus' battle when he will cast them in to the sea of fire."

She tried to focus on Bob's face, but found herself drifting again and again into prayer. Bob knew she was praying and said nothing, hoping to join her at some point. "Jesus is our strength, our provider, our Lord," she whispered.

"I can do all things through Christ who strengthens me," Bob extolled. "I am a conquer in Christ Jesus," he continued.

They would pray often, for the word of God is power for the pulling down of strongholds. Their friends would pray with them and for them. Some would learn the power and presence of prayer when placed before God. Others would learn the power of being a child of God. The Word of God spoken from them would train and teach many how to place their love and hope in Christ. Christ dwelt within their hearts; The Holy Spirit would make the Spirit-to-Spirit connection with God. They knew God; they were the works of His hands. Together they prayed the prayer of faith, the prayer of forgiveness of sin. Together they prayed.

Ready to write?

Today's Date:

_____

_____

_____

_____

_____

_____

_____

_____

_____

15 HOW DOES A DISCIPLE PETITION GOD?

Purpose:
To make your requests known to God.

Hearing the Word:
Philippians 4:6-9
"Do not be anxious about anything, but in every situation, by prayer and petition, with thanksgiving, present your requests to God. And the peace of God, which transcends all understanding, will guard your hearts and your minds in Christ Jesus.

Finally, brothers and sisters, whatever is true, whatever is noble, whatever is right, whatever is pure, whatever is lovely, whatever is admirable—if anything is excellent or praiseworthy—think about such things. Whatever you have learned or received or heard from me, or seen in me—put it into practice. And the God of peace will be with you. Prayer is simply communication with God. It requires speaking to and listening to God. Believers can pray from the heart, freely, spontaneously, and in their own words. There are no correct words, scripts or postures for prayer."

Matthew 6:7 NIV
"When you pray, don't babble on and on as people of other religions do. They think their prayers are answered only by repeating their words again and again."

To Petition is to make or present a formal request to an authority with respect to a particular cause. A petition requires some action be taken. A request is a petition. Prayer is the way to petition God, but it is not the only way. Prayer is a way to communicate with God. Petitions are delivered as prayer, but there are other forms of prayer (glorification, confession, thanksgiving) that are not petitions.

Philippians 4:6-9 is a prayer and a petition. Disciples petition God by letting our request be known to Him. We are to give God praise, worship and thanksgiving. God will supply our every need, but we are to go before God with humility. Petitions are requests.

Story:

Devon thought it best that he place his petition before God, because his inability to deal with a tragedy that caused so many problems in his life. He had prayed and prayed gently and lovingly before God, but thought a stronger request for action was necessary since he had not heard from God. He cleared his prayer closet of everything but his Bible and prayer cloth and began a conversation with God about his situation. The lawyer in Devon led him to lay out all the specifics of his request. He thought out every step of the process, even wrote it down, to not forget any phase of the request. He knew God was able to grant his request and he knew that only God could make this happen.

Devon had lead a quiet life, a humble life and had served God for many years in many ways for his church. Today he would petition God to spare his son's life. He had all the details of what he was going to say about life and love. He believed God would hear his prayer. He was willing to give himself, to allow is son to live. His request was not complex or difficult to carry out. God, he thought, this is reasonable. He had talked it through with several people who felt he was way out of alignment with his request. His petition required a direct response from God and his faith said all things are possible and God would agree to his request. So he entered his prayer closet and prayed. Calling upon God for mercy, grace and favor. He humbled himself as best he could. Drained of all energy, having spent his voice as he placed his request, Devon concluded his request. He now had to wait, he knew in his heart that God loved him and would answer.

Ready to write?

Today's Date:

_____

_____

_____

_____

_____

_____

_____

_____

_____

_____

_____

16 WHAT SHOULD A DISCIPLE LEAVE BEHIND?

Purpose:
To exemplify Christ through our lifestyles.

Hearing the Word:
Ephesians 4:22-24
"You were taught, with regard to your former way of life, to put off your old self, which is being corrupted by its deceitful desires; to be made new in the attitude of your minds; and to put on the new self, created to be like God in true righteousness and holiness."

Romans 10:9, states that, if you declare with your mouth, "Jesus is Lord," and believe in your heart that God raised him from the dead, you will be saved. Though primary this should be the confession and accepting Jesus as Lord, moves one from the world to the disciple role. The declaration with your mouth that Jesus is Lord and that one believes with the heart that God raised him from the dead, ends with salvation. The ways of the world should be forsaken and the new creature in Christ should begin to emerge. Ephesians 4:22-24 takes the disciple into putting off the things of the world and truly focusing on God. The deceitful desires are replaced with the new character of the fruit of The Spirit as Jesus shared with His disciples that The Holy Spirit would come and a baptism with fire would be eminent. There is no longer a place for the deceitful desires of the world. The old sinful man is replaced with the new man and seeks to move closer to God. The sins of the eyes of the flesh, lust of the flesh and pride of life no longer control the new convert. The old morals, habits and beliefs in the worldly system are replaced and sanctification is gained. The new man puts on goodness and a renewed righteous mind taking on a new image of God. The spirit of the new man can commune with the Spirit of God in truth. This newness of life brings about a new attitude and holiness.

Story:

Brian's baptism happened thirty years ago when he was 12. It was customary at his church that the process take place. Brian attended church with his parents to see his friends. He never took church seriously and when he turned 18 he walked away. As time moved on Brian found himself repeating the process which he had been exposed to of going to church just for going to church's sake. Things have changed slightly, now Brain was taking his children to church. He quite often remembered the complaints that he had shared with his parents of being bored.

The one thing Brian found enjoyable this time around was telling his children about his church antics. It was enough to get them into the church building. Brian noticed, however, that his oldest daughter was getting involved with the youth team and studied for Sunday school services. His youngest Nate was involved with the tot program and enjoyed giving his Sunday school report on what he had learned in class. His wife Natalie was involved with the Missionary Society. Brian found himself right back where he had left off 18 year ago. He had no excitement about the Sunday trips to church. He knew very little about the Sunday school lessons yet he hungered to make the changes in himself to seek God. He did not remember how that was supposed to happen. What he had noticed is that the other men in church seemed more in tune with the service than he did. There was a deep desire to have his whole family involved and growing in Christ.

One Sunday Brian took the plunge and stood before the congregation and told of his desire to get to know Christ. He felt sad to have to confess not having paid attention in the past, but wanted to have Jesus in his life and the lives of all his family members. He fought the old man who wanted to stay in the world. There were changes to be made in his private life that he was willing to undergo and his family helped. What he found was a church also willing to help him along the way. The men's ministry was open about some of the activities that Brian had to give up and they welcomed him, but not his worldly ways. Brian had to put the old man to rest. Others had been through the same process and would mentor Brian through his difficult times.

The Pastor suggested a biblically based reading plan, more involvement in Bible Study and a buddy system to help when the need arose for additional support. Brian started in the youth class with his youngest child. It opened up conversations with his family that they had not known before. His daughter was excited when he moved up to the youth study program. Baptism day was a family event.

The day Brian joined the adult class was celebrated by the entire congregation, but fell short of the grand excitement that filled the church on the day Brian taught the adult study group.

Ready to write?

Today's Date:

_____

_____

_____

_____

_____

_____

_____

_____

_____

_____

_____

_____

_____

_____

_____

_____

_____

Dr. Amanda Goodson

17 WHAT DOES AN OBEDIENT DISCIPLE GAIN?

Purpose:

To walk in divine peace and reap the harvest.

Hearing the Word:

Deuteronomy 11:1-15

"Love the Lord your God and keep his requirements, his decrees, his laws and his commands always. Remember today that your children were not the ones who saw and experienced the discipline of the Lord your God: his majesty, his mighty hand, his outstretched arm; the signs he performed and the things he did in the heart of Egypt, both to Pharaoh king of Egypt and to his whole country; what he did to the Egyptian army, to its horses and chariots, how he overwhelmed them with the waters of the

Red Sea as they were pursuing you, and how the Lord brought lasting ruin on them. It was not your children who saw what he did for you in the wilderness until you arrived at this place, and what he did to Dathan and Abiram, sons of Eliab the Reubenite, when the earth opened its mouth right in the middle of all Israel and swallowed them up with their households, their tents and every living thing that belonged to them. But it was your own eyes that saw all these great things the Lord has done.

Observe therefore all the commands I am giving you today, so that you may have the strength to go in and take over the land that you are crossing the Jordan to possess, and so that you may live long in the land the Lord swore to your ancestors to give to them and their descendants, a land flowing with milk and honey. The land you are entering to take over is not like the land of Egypt, from which you have come, where you planted your seed and irrigated it by foot as in a vegetable garden. But the land you are crossing the Jordan to take possession of is a land of mountains and valleys that drinks rain from heaven. It is a land the Lord your God cares for; the eyes of the Lord your God are continually on it from the beginning of the year to its end.

So if you faithfully obey the commands I am giving you today—to love the Lord your God and to serve him with all your heart and with all your soul—then I will send rain on your land in its season, both autumn and spring rains, so that you may gather in your grain, new wine and olive oil. I will provide grass in the fields for your cattle, and you will eat and be satisfied.

Deuteronomy 28:1-14

If you fully obey the LORD your God and carefully follow all his commands I give you today, the LORD your God will set you high above all the nations on earth. All these blessings will come on you and accompany you if you obey the LORD your God: You will be blessed in the city and blessed in the country. The fruit of your womb will be blessed, and the crops of your land and the young of your livestock—the calves of your herds and the lambs of your flocks. Your basket and your kneading trough will be blessed. You will be blessed when you come in and blessed when you go out. The LORD will grant that the enemies who rise up against you will be defeated before you. They will come at you from one direction but flee from you in seven.

The LORD will send a blessing on your barns and on everything you put your hand to. The LORD your God will bless you in the land he is giving you. The LORD will establish you as his holy people, as he promised you on oath, if you keep the commands of the LORD your God and walk in obedience to him. Then all the peoples on earth will see that you are called by the name of the LORD, and they will fear you. The LORD will grant you abundant prosperity—in the fruit of your womb, the young of your livestock and the crops of your ground—in the land he swore to your ancestors to give you.

The LORD will open the heavens, the storehouse of his bounty, to send rain on your land in season and to bless all the work of your hands. You will lend to many nations but will borrow from none. The LORD will make you the head, not the tail. If you pay attention to the commands of the LORD your God that I give you this day and carefully follow them, you will always be at the top, never at the bottom. Do not turn aside from any of the commands I give you today, to the right or to the left, following other gods and serving them.

Story:

Tiffani pleaded with her Mom to let her drive the family van. She had watched her Dad drive and in three years would have her license. Dad had let her drive the car up the street several times. She could do it.

Every day the same request to drive, every day Mom had given her the same reasoning for the emphatic "No," she received. Mom explained the danger of not knowing the law was only one reason for "No" and to support the "NO," all the "what if" possibilities lined up next:

- What if you get into an accident!
- What if you hurt someone!
- What if you crash the van!

Tiffani did not want to hear the reasons again, so one evening she took her Mother's keys and headed out the door. She and her little sister proceeded to back the van out of the driveway. Within moments of taking the keys, Heather ran into the house to let their Mom know that Tiffani had backed into a tree and the van was lodged against it so that it would not move. Tiffani set in the car crying.

Mom looked at the passenger side door, gave Tiffani a sheet of paper and pen, and told her to mathematically figure out how to move the van away from the tree. It was simple geometry. She told Heather that she had to help Tiffani figure out the angles in which to move the van using the tree as the point of reference. Heather started to cry. About an hour later, they came into the house with their equations. It will work if you turn the wheel in this direction at this angle. If I turn the wheel, Mom asked? Your plan, you carry it out, while I explain to your Father what happened and let him know that you have it under control.

Both children headed reluctantly out the door. Both sat in the van and cried. Mom and Dad talked. Dad voted for capital punishment. In their house capital punishment was a whipping, which was Dad's responsibility to carry out, because Mon did not embrace such punishment. Mom told Dad that she did not foresee the incident occurring again. She shared a more intense list of "what ifs'" with him. Dad knew the law. Tiffani knew that the law did not allow her to drive for three more years. Allowing her to do so was unlawful and all the "what if's," became possibilities. Mom called the children in to eat, but no one had an appetite. All four family members had learned a harsh lesson that breaking the law at any time was not good.

God so loved the world that He gave His only begotten Son…shall not perish. Jesus said, "I came to fulfill the law not to do away with it. Tiffani waited three years to fulfill the law.

Disciples learn to emulate Christ and receive the blessings!

Ready to write?

Today's Date:

_____

_____

_____

_____

_____

_____

_____

_____

_____

_____

_____

_____

_____

_____

Dr. Amanda Goodson

18 HOW SHOULD A DISCIPLE RELATE TO CHRIST?

Purpose:
To always follow Christ's example as teacher.

Hearing the Word:

Luke 6:40
"The student is not above the teacher, but everyone who is fully trained will be like their teacher."

1 Corinthians 11:1
Follow my example, as I follow the example of Christ.

Story:

As children, our first role model is usually a parent or a teacher. Teachers have the special position of instilling in us the intellectual world. Julie knew that she would someday be a teacher. Her favorite teacher was Mrs. Williams, who had this crazy saying, "My stars are blue." Mrs. Williams made class fun and easy to learn. All who met her liked her and she took great pride in the success of her students.

After, graduation, Julie was assigned to Provost Elementary School. The times had changed and Julie found that the students were very different from her youthful days. Their level of enthusiasm was very different. The classroom diversity was very new to Julie and interacting with her students often required the presence of a second teacher or parent. Julie remembered how Mrs. Williams had held their interest. No new-fangled gadgets to contend with and somehow the classes seemed smaller, twenty-eight students every day was sometimes overwhelming.

What Julie did remember, with joy, was the ridiculous songs Mrs. Williams sang with them every morning. She also remembers the joy of positive reinforcement for the smallest accomplishment. One very hectic morning Julie burst out into a song about eating worms. At first the kids were stunned as she did not look at anyone in particular, but proceeded as if she had actually swallowed a worm. It was hilarious, almost as funny as when Mrs. Williams had performed the same song. The children began to look forward to learning new songs and Julie had a whole book full of them. The songs seemed to settle the kids down and put them in a more receptive mood for the rest of the day. Though she pondered over it for a long time, Julie never figured why Mrs. Williams would yell out at the end of every song, "My Stars Are Blue!"

Jesus did not aspire to be greater than or equal to God. Christ set the standard for discipleship. He was preacher, teacher, and counselor to the disciples. It is evident as we read The Bible that these traits are seen in Peter and James. At some time in space, a student becomes a teacher and he must always remember (like Paul) that he was once a student.

Ready to write?

Today's Date:

_____

_____

_____

_____

_____

_____

_____

Dr. Amanda Goodson

19 WHAT IS THE IMAGE OF A DISCIPLE?

Purpose:
To reflect Jesus Christ.

Hearing the Word:

Romans 8:28-29
"And we know that in all things God works for the good of those who love him, who have been called according to his purpose. For those God foreknew he also predestined to be conformed to the image of his Son, that he might be the firstborn among many brothers and sisters."

All things God works for the good of these who love him. Note in this part of the passage that God is doing the work. God works all things for the good of those who love him. The work is being done for the good of those who love God. For those God foreknew (had previous knowledge of) He also predestined (someone for a particular fate or purpose) to be conformed (to give the same shape, outline, or contour to: bring into harmony or accord) to the image of His Son, that He might be the firstborn among many brothers and sisters:

2 Timothy 1:9
"Who hath saved us, and called us with an holy calling, not according to our works, but according to his own purpose and grace, which was given us in Christ Jesus before the world began."

Acts 1:8
"But you will receive power when the Holy Spirit comes on you; and you will be my witnesses in Jerusalem, and in all Judea and Samaria, and <u>to</u> the ends of the earth."

Paul explains in the prayer of Colossians 1:15-20 (NIV), The Son is the image of the invisible God, the firstborn over all creation. For in Him all things were created: things in heaven and on earth, visible and invisible, whether thrones or powers or rulers or authorities; all things have been created through Him and for Him. He is before all things, and in Him all things hold together. And He is the head of The Body, The Church; He is the beginning and the firstborn from among the dead, so that in everything He might have supremacy. For God was pleased to have all His fullness dwell in Him, and through Him to reconcile to Himself all things, whether things on earth or things in heaven, by making peace through His blood, shed on the cross. Therefore, the image of a disciple of God is the image of Jesus Christ. The work of a disciple of God is the work of Jesus Christ. Matthew 28:19 (NIV), "Therefore go and make disciples of all nations, baptizing them in the name of the Father and of the Son and of The Holy Spirit."

Story:

When Steve joined his new church the congregation was all aglow about the new training classes on discipleship. He was excited because he knew God and Jesus as his Lord and Savior. His church history was extensive and he understood that the new training was going to be intensive. He was ready for the challenge. He wanted everyone that he knew to know the love, grace and power of God and God's Word. He was excited that his discipleship and evangelizing skills would be stretched to new heights and explore new ways to help make his challenge come to life. The first year of training was more self-realization of the power to "make" disciples and grow his church was within Steve's grasp. He learned about discipleship, evangelizing, exhorting and generally how to redefine one's concept of "church."

Church, he now understood, was not a club membership and he was not just a "church" member, but an ambassador and disciple called and equipped to do work. Steve was not an island; everyone in the church was responsible for making disciples. His skills were improved weekly. The pastor delivered a powerful message from God every week; Steve's knowledge was enhanced in Bible Study (on his own and in groups) and through Sunday school involvement and activities. There were opportunities to grow in his prayer life and his praise and worship of God. Steve looked around his community and saw that the harvest was plenty, but the workers were few. He smiled at the thought that his observations simply meant that he would have to reap a little more and work a little harder. As for the workers and harvest, Steve knew God would provide the increase. For many the Apostle Paul had given the best explanation of how to harvest new disciples in 1 Corinthians 3:6-7, 23, when he explained how the Lord assigns each his role:

"I planted the seed, Apollos watered it, but God has been making it grow. So neither the one who plants nor the one who waters is anything, but only God, who makes things grow… and you are of Christ, and Christ is of God."

As Trinity Temple Church we have been elevated in 2017! The plan for the New Year includes more intense training on discipleship!

Ready to write?

Today's Date:

_____

_____

_____

_____

_____

_____

_____

_____

_____

_____

_____

_____

_____

_____

20 WHAT IS THE PATTERN OF A DISCIPLE?

Purpose:

To use Christ as a model for life.

Hearing the Word:

Philippians 3:17

"Join together in following my example, brothers and sisters, and just as you have us as a model, keep your eyes on those who live as we do."

A pattern is just an organized plan on how to approach a situation.

Story:

Paul displays a confidence in the success of other disciples who followed Jesus as a pattern to live and worship God by. It has worked for Christ and will work for those dedicated to taking up their crosses and following Him. Love, obedience and submission are three of the keys to discipleship. Can you name others?

Joshua was called according to God's purpose to replace Moses and lead the Israelites into the new land. The genius of Joshua's plan was that all of his victory included God. He obeyed the instructions that were given to him, which guaranteed the outcome. nThe same God who guaranteed Joshua's success in battle sent His son as a pattern for future disciples to follow and change lives for kingdom people. God told Joshua to have the armed men march around the city once each day, for six days. The priests were to carry the ark, blowing trumpets, but the soldiers were to keep silent. On the seventh day, the assembly marched around the walls of Jericho seven times. Joshua told them that by God's order, every living thing in the city must be destroyed, except Rahab and her family.

At Joshua's command, the men gave a great shout, and Jericho's walls fell down flat! The Israelite army rushed in and took over the city. Only Rahab and her family were spared.

Joshua followed the pattern that God had given him. He knew that Moses had submitted and followed God's orders very well. Joshua carried out the plan just as God had laid it out before him and the nation of Israel.

2 Corinthians 3:18

"And we all, who with unveiled faces contemplate the Lord's glory, are being transformed into his image with ever-increasing glory, which comes from the Lord, who is the Spirit."

God is Spirit and we worship him in spirit and in truth. We grow as we come to understand and walk in the purpose of God. We no longer need to worry about sending someone behind the veil to represent us, we have the freedom to worship God in spirit and in truth. Can you imagine being worried about what you say, what you do, what you look like, what you wear and what you are to eat?

As detailed in the book of Genesis we were created in God's image.

"Then God said, 'Let Us make man in Our image, according to Our likeness.' God created man in His own image, in the image of God He created him; male and female He created them." We regain our status and rebirth in Christ. Read also Matthew 6:31-35, which instructs us to not worry about these things. "So do not worry, saying, 'What shall we eat?' or 'What shall we drink?' or 'What shall we wear?' For the pagans run after all these things, and your heavenly Father knows that you need them. But seek first His kingdom and His righteousness, and all these things will be given to you as well. Do not worry about tomorrow, for tomorrow will take care of itself. Each day has enough trouble of its own."

This is the knowledge of every disciple: we are transformed by renewing our minds, thoughts and actions in every life situation.

Ready to write?

Today's Date:

_____

_____

_____

_____

_____

_____

_____

_____

_____

_____

21 WHAT IS THE REWARD OF A DISCIPLE?

Purpose:
To know that we are doing the will of Christ.

Hearing the Word:

Romans 8:37-39
"No, in all these things we are more than conquerors through him who loved us. For I am convinced that neither death nor life, neither angels nor demons, neither the present nor the future, nor any powers, neither height nor depth, nor anything else in all creation, will be able to separate us from the love of God that is in Christ Jesus our Lord."

Story:

Rosa arrived in this country snug and secure in her father's arms. Her mother and brothers had been separated from the two of them for several days. Years later when she could understand the tragic event, her father would tell her how her mother and brothers had been left behind. The evacuation had taken place with very little notice or time to gather the family or their few belongings. The crowds of people had pushed frantically forward so that many were displaced or lost in the crowd. The long trip to safety had seemed months and endless, her father would add. The story made him sad that all of his family had not made it to safety. Years had passed before word came that her mother and brothers were not able to make it to the evacuation point. They had remained behind in a war torn country that did not want them, but they were not harmed. Rosa longed to meet her mother and brothers for she was an infant when this all occurred. She and her father had reached safety, but were held in camp for an additional year before finding their way to a safe haven.

Rosa grew up with the love of her father and the longing for her mother. At thirty years of age she began to plot her return to her native country to look for her mother. She was not sure how to do this or if she could. She was determined to try. No U.S.

citizens were allowed to return. The trip would be expensive, but the cost of not trying was greater.

Rosa explained her desire to her church that pledged to help support her as well as they could. Their greatest asset was prayer. They formed a prayer group that met twice a week and prayed that God would help Rosa find her family. Acquiring the funds took another three years.

Now thirty-three, Rosa had applied to the government for permission to return, but was denied. She never gave up hope and prayed consistently that she would someday be allowed to return to find her family. At the 40th anniversary of her leaving, the government of the two countries decided to open up trade negations. Finally the tourist industry was allowed to accept people for visits. Rosa applied and was approved. For the first time since her early childhood Rosa would step on native soil.

She followed instructions, and trails outlined for her from people who remembered the old country, telling her to go here and not there. With the help of many people from both countries Rosa found her brothers. She met them for the first time, but she did not meet her mother. They laughed together and cried together. Her brothers told her stories of their mother and how she loved Rosa and prayed for her well-being at all times. Her intense sense of loss for the mother she longed to meet was quenched by the stories of love and longing that her brothers poured into her. The vast emptiness for her mother was somewhat dulled by the overwhelming love she encountered from family she had never known. Although she had never visited the country, her father's memory of it had kept them both close to it. The grace and love of God and His love for all of His children had crossed thousands of miles and years and held the family together.

Ready to write?

Today's Date:

_____

_____

_____

_____

_____

_____

_____

_____

_____

CONCLUSION

As I stated in the first part of this book - God, as our heavenly Father, wants to teach us about His way, will and desire for our lives. From the moment that God gives us His breath of life, we have the opportunity to experience oneness with Him and we can learn more about Him every day. My desire for you as a disciple (follower and student) is to know God better and acknowledge Him as Lord.

This book, *Drawn to Discipleship,* has given you a daily roadmap to becoming a more devoted learner and follower of Christ. It has brought you to a position where you can reach a heightened awareness where divine learning, impartation and inspiration though prayer reside. Every learner should desire to pray better and become comfortable doing so every day.

I trust this daily walk has gently guided you in taking a practical and applicable journey of followership to reach Christ's goal for all to know God. The intent of this book, as with my other 21 Days of Prayer books, was that you were able to accomplish this by utilizing relevant stories that demonstrate how to live and are made better because of a true relationship with Jesus Christ the Savior.

I am encouraged that you have taken this daily journey and have seen how your life can and will be transformed through prayer. It is guaranteed that, through a daily commitment to prayer, your life will be changed, your relationship with God will be enhanced, and you will see the difference this makes in your life. Believe it and be "Drawn to Discipleship"!

END NOTES

Chapter 1

[1] New International Version Bible. Zondervan
[2] NIV The Learning Bible:
[3] The American Heritage College Dictionary 4th Addition. Houghton Mifflin Company. Boston*New York
[4] Ibid
[5] Easton's Bible Dictionary v1.0. 2008, 2009 AcroDesign Technologies.
[6] Google Translate
[7] New International Version of The Bible: Matthew 10:2
[8] The Bible: NIV

Chapter 2

[9] The American Heritage College Dictionary. 4th Edition. Houghton Mifflin Company. Boston * New York p35.
[10] Ibid
[11] NIV Study Bible (Matthew 11:27).
[12] The American Heritage College Dictionary. 4th Edition. Houghton Mifflin Company. Boston * New York.
[13] NIV Study Bible Matthew 10:5-7
[14] NIV Study Bible

Chapter 4

[15] The New Interpreter's Study Bible. New Revised Standard Version with the Apocrypha 2003. Abingdon Press. Nashville. 1806
[16] Ibid. 1764.

Chapter 5

[17] NIV Study Bible
[18] Ibid
[19] Easton's Bible Dictionary v1.0. 2008, 2009. Acro Design Technologies, Dictionary Topics from M.G. Easton's Illustrated Bible Dictionary

Chapter 6

[20] Easton's Bible Dictionary v1.0 Copyright 2008, 2009. AcroDesign technologies, www.acrodesigntech.com. Dictionary Topics from M.G. Easton's illustrated Bible Dictionary.

Chapter 7

[21] NIV Bible
[22] NIV Bible

Chapter 8

[23] New International Interprets Bible.
[24] www.biblestudytools.com

Chapter 9

[25] NIV Bible

Chapter 10

[26] Easton's bible dictionary

ABOUT THE AUTHOR

Dr. Amanda H. Goodson

Amanda is an author, educator, facilitator, inspirational speaker and coach for corporations, agencies and non-profit organizations. Amanda inspires others and connects with her audiences by sharing real-life experiences using enthusiastic, energizing, and interactive methods. Amanda has a Bachelor's of Science in Electrical Engineering, a Master's of Science in Management, and a Doctor of Ministry Church Administration.

For further information or to book Dr. Goodson please contact her at:

AmandaGoodson.com

Books by Dr. Amanda Goodson

Spiritual Quickbooks ™

Kingdom Character

Spiritual Authority

Carmel Voices

The Power to Make an Impact

Powerful People Follow Christ

Step out in Faith

Going Higher, Declarations for Kids

On the Rise

Spiritual Intelligence

Switch to Holiness

12 Power Principles for Kingdom Leaders

Leadership Minibooks ™

The Authority of a Leader

Character of a Leader

Unlock Your Full Potential

12 Power Principles for Administrative Professionals

Soar to Your Destiny

Dr. Amanda Goodson

Leadership Workbooks

Switch to Holiness Workbook

Unlock Your Full Potential Workbook

Soar to Your Destiny Workbook

12 Power Principles for Kingdom Leaders Workbook

PersonalSanctuary™ GoodTinybooks™

Victory – 30 days of Meditation

Fruitful – 30 Days of Meditation

Success – 30 Days of Affirmations

Influence – 30 days of Affirmations